WITHDRAWN

Bridgton & Saco River Railroad.

WARNING.

For some time past, the officers of the Railroad, passengers and others have been greatly annoyed by the crowd of idlers and loafers who have gathered in crowds at the Stations and Grounds of the Company on arrival of trains. These crowds of loafers have become a nuisance and will not be tolerated longer. For the benefit of

Chapter 51. Section 79, Revised Statutes, reads as follows:

No person shall loiter or remain without right within any car or stationhouse of a Railroad Corporation or Steamboat, or upon the platforms or grounds adjoining such Station after being requested to leave the same by any Railroad officer, or officer or agent of such steamboat. Whoever violates this section forfeits not less than two nor more than ten dollars to be recovered on complaint.

People who have business with the railroad or its agents are welcome at all times.

Idlers and loafers will not be tolerated and if they do not keep away from the Stations and Grounds will be prosecuted.

J. A. Bennett, Supt.

"BUSTED

AND STILL RUNNING"

Glistening with factory paint, B&SR No. 7 ready to leave Harrison

"BUSTED AND STILL RUNNING"

The Famous Two-Foot Gauge Railroad of Bridgton, Maine

EDGAR T. MEAD, JR.

1968   **THE STEPHEN GREENE PRESS**   Brattleboro, Vermont

*Near Perley's Mills,
No. 8 pads noiselessly along
the snowcovered way*

Photo Credits

EDWARD BOND: photographs reproduced on pages 18, 19, 22 top, 27 and half-title, 28, 31, 32, 41; and (in data section) No. 6 and load, Smoker No. 25, Coach No. 15, and narrow-gauge tank cars. E. H. BROWN: page 53 bottom. MAINE HISTORICAL SOCIETY COLLECTION: pages 10, 11, 13, 20. RAIL PHOTO SERVICE (from Cornwall-Martin Collection): page 31. Others, EDGAR T. MEAD, JR.

Book, cover, and jacket design by Russel Hamilton. Composed and printed by The Vermont Printing Company, Brattleboro.

INTRODUCTION

COME WITH US for a little while to the gravelly hills and pine bordered ponds of Maine where a short narrow gauge railroad dared to elbow its way through the primeval forest between Bridgton and Hiram in deepest Cumberland County. Memories of the little line are growing fainter, even as the right of way succumbs to second growth brush and the erosion of Time, and it is past due to recall the hopes and glories of another day.

Narrow-gauge land was peopled by witty, friendly, patient folk as I grew to know them during school vacations as a railroadical man-of-all-work, finally ending as Superintendent at the tender age of 19. No doubt my official reports are still treasured archivally at the I.C.C. in Washington, and I chuckle about that. Sipping a sodapop "tonic" whenever there was time to sit and talk, one quickly absorbed those salty oaths and Down East mannerisms. "By gory, you're quite a cuttah" was standard speech, echoing ancestral sounds of the Yankee countryside. Personalities, blasphemy and the latest off-color jokes imported from Portland, these were the conversation of the Narrow Gauge. It was all this and more, for $18 per week.

Linwood Moody, Temple Crittenden, Scott Thomas, Newell Martin and Hugh Boutell were my original mentors on narrow-gauge matters and for original research I must also thank Bill McLin, who with Bob Dingley and myself compiled a now out-of-

v

print monograph on the line. The Maine Historical Society, Ed Bond, Scott Dawson, Glenn Davis and Rail Photo Service supplied previously unpublished illustrations along with several from my own collection. My agreeable editors and proofreaders included Charles E. Fisher, Linwood Moody, Temple Crittenden, Wes Griswold, Russ Hamilton and Jan Greene.

Edgar T. Mead, Jr.
1158 Fifth Avenue

Bridgton & Saco River Railroad.
Good for ONE PASSAGE from
BRIDGTON JUNC.
—TO—
BRIDGTON
5112

THE LONG MAINE WINTER of 1883 had been an off-again-on-again kind of season, and in the country village of Bridgton on January 21st the skies were dull gray once more. After a week of thaw, it looked as though another snowstorm was on the way.

There was good reason for the locals to poke out-of-doors on this particular Saturday. Joe Bennett had promised that the inaugural steam train would reach town that day, and "firsts" of such magnitude were rare indeed in Bridgton. Early shoppers had stopped by the ornate little station on newly christened Depot Street, and the word they passed along was that the train ought to arrive during the afternoon. Track-laying had started on the 16-mile narrow-gauge railroad during the preceding summer. Expectable delays had postponed completion until the latter part of January, a cruel month for building track—or anything else, for that matter.

After lunch on January 21st, residents of upper and lower Bridgton, and even a few from North Bridgton and Highland Lake, began to gather around the station grounds. Tethered horses, wisps of steam from their blanketed backs sharply visible in the cold air, greeted newcomers with snorts of welcome. Grown-ups conversed in huddles, silencing themselves almost as if at command whenever a childish shout sounded like a far-off train whistle or the stamp of a hoof was mistaken for the distant beat of an engine's exhaust. The usual cynical grunts of disbelief were voiced, and good-natured joshing was directed at the businessmen and other local gentry whose hearts and wallets had been invested in Bridgton's iron route to the outside world. Why a narrow-gauge railroad? What if it failed?

Early arrivals had a long, chilly wait, for it was nearly five o'clock when suddenly, down by the Willett Road crossing, a series of staccato whistle blasts demanded the full attention of everyone within earshot. Children stopped their play. Their elders turned to face the whistling. Then there was silence, an eerie silence damped by snow. As the crowd strained to listen, the rapid panting of the tiny approaching engine's exhaust broke the stillness and rapidly became the one sound that dominated all others. It rose in volume, then abruptly stopped as Engineer John Marque slowed for one of the inevitable sags created as the result of hasty cutting and filling for roadbed. A joyous chatter swept the gathering, now fast swelling as belated townspeople heard the shrill whistle and whipped their horses down to the station grounds.

Cheers mounted as the little black engine first came within sight, hull-down on the landscape, rocking side to side, belching great plumes of smoke. Its several cars bucked and swayed in a kind of sinuous dance. As the engine drew near, the steam of its brake and steam from its pop valves saluted the crowd in a flourish of victory. Metallic sounds of the little train mingled with hand-clapping, shouts, laughter, bell-ringing, and general uproar. The Bridgton Cornet Band, Frankie Cash conducting, broke into a lively medley. Local dignitaries—including John Mead, sign painter, taxidermist and president of the Literary Association—waved their hats enthusiastically. Horses reared. Children shrieked. The narrow-gauge train had arrived at last, and it would stay for many prosperous years—and several lean years.

The new railroad, with its toy-like 24-inch gauge, was Bridgton's up-to-date substitute for a canal that it had once had, and lost.

IN 1820, when Maine advanced to statehood from its former condition of being the private northern reserve of Massachusetts, the merchants, sawyers, and farmers of upper Cumberland County were most thankful. They hoped the new state capital at Portland would listen closely to their needs for efficient transportation. It did. In 1821, the Cumberland & Oxford Canal was chartered. Canal boats were destined to start at Waterford, a thriving village north of Harrison and Bridgton, and be towed through Long Pond, the Songo River, Lake Sebago, and an excavated canal to Portland. Promoters planned to obtain $50,000 toward an estimated cost of $137,000 from a lottery, and the balance from the Canal Bank of Portland and local investors. When completed in 1830 at a final cost of over $200,000, the project comprised 18 miles of dug canal, 20 miles of natural waterway through the lakes, and 27 locks, contributing to a vertical lift of 300 feet. Before long, a hundred flat-bottomed boats swelled the budding fleet. An important customer was the shipping industry, which sought giant first-growth pines for masts from "that steadfast legion of stalwart knights in dominant empery" standing in ranks on the sandy knolls of Cumberland County.

Steamboating came to the rivers and lakes when the impressively named Sebago & Long Pond Steam Navigation Company was founded in 1846. The management's first frail steamer, *Fawn,* puffed three times a week from Harrison via Bridgton to the canal entrance on Lake Sebago. From that point, freight could be barged through the canal, while impatient passengers took the speedier stagecoach for Portland. Industry and commerce blossomed slowly in Maine's cold climate; for every resident who stayed, another decided to turn to the Great West, there to build a home and fortune.

Maine's pulse beat more quickly after the Civil War, when young men returned from distant states with stored-up ambition and accumulated experience. The war established railroading as the great sinew of modern American commerce, and rail lines were soon projected up and down every important valley. Following along the Saco River Valley came the Portland & Ogdensburg Railroad, eastern link in a long-distance scheme to chain the granaries beyond the Great Lakes with Portland's all-season deep harbor. Shortly before had come the Atlantic & St. Lawrence Railroad, a British plot to circumnavigate the frozen St. Lawrence River to transport grain shipments from Montreal to Portland. As a result of these developments, the stage lines were forced to focus attention on building feeder routes. As still another consequence of rail service to Sebago, the wonderful old canal closed forever in the year 1870.

If the coming of the standard-gauge railroad was death to canals, it seemed to breathe new life into steamboating. A spanking new sidewheeler was soon placed in service on Lake Sebago, under the command of Captain Symonds. Its name, *Oriental,* was no doubt a reflection of Maine's gradual awareness of the wide world, which it served both by great clipper ships and by westerly bands of steel rails. *Oriental* was followed by *Sebago* and *Mt. Pleasant,* and passengers and freight along the lakes soon grew dependent on the expanded service.

3

Unfortunately, "when the year was in its yellowing time," the face of Nature signaled the start of human hibernation until March and the ice retreat. For Bridgton, formerly the village of Pondicherry, located between Long Pond and Highland Lake, abandonment of the canal, not to mention winter cessation of steamboat service and consequent dependence on the hard mercies of teamsters and stage lines, was intolerable. Angered but still buoyantly optimistic, the citizens of Bridgton gradually began to believe that salvation lay in building their own railroad to the outside world.

For a town of a few thousand inhabitants, construction of a railroad loomed as an almost insurmountable task. Bridgton's wealth was invested in the soil and in merchants' inventories, not idle cash. The venture capital of New York, Boston, and Europe was intent upon developing the West.

Stephenson's popular gauge of 4 feet, 8½ inches, had been selected for main-line railroads in Britain, on the Continent, and in the United States, but contemporary engineering opinion argued that a narrower width was perhaps more suitable for branches. Charles E. Spooner, designer of the successful Festiniog Railway in Wales, sowed a new philosophy with his book *Narrow Gauge Railways*. A lively crop of narrow-gauge fans sprang up, led by British engineer Robert Fairlie, whose enthusiasm in turn influenced the Duke of Sutherland to construct a 3-foot-gauge line on the Isle of Man. A visitor from America, General William Jackson Palmer, youthful Civil War hero, watched and studied, and returned home to Colorado fired with a plan to build railroads of 3-foot gauge from there all the way to Mexico and the Pacific Ocean. Bridgton heard about the narrow-gauge theory, and on February 14, 1873, there appeared an article in the local paper stating that for half the $30,000-per-mile estimated cost of standard gauge, Bridgton could build its own 3-foot-gauge railroad.

The Panic of 1873 and a business recession lasting through 1878 produced ill effects on Bridgton as well as elsewhere, and railroad plans were shelved for several years. Narrow-gauge railroading in Maine received its first important boost from an 1879 plan to construct a line with a 2-foot gauge in Franklin County. Named the Sandy River Railroad, it was to connect the standard gauge at Farmington with the towns of Strong and Phillips, budding gateways to large timber reserves. Its promoter was George E. Mansfield of Boston, who, like General Palmer, had visited the fifteen-year-old Festiniog and returned from Wales bursting with desire to create similar branch lines in America.

In 1875 Mansfield surveyed and constructed an 8-mile railroad

4

The eyes of narrow-gauge promoters popped when they saw the Festiniog Fairlie engines make short work of the Welsh mountains

between Bedford on the Middlesex Central Railroad, and North Billerica on the Boston, Lowell & Nashua Railroad. The demonstration line opened with a flourish of two tiny locomotives and eleven cars in November 1877. Although an engineering success, the fledgling Billerica & Bedford was snuffed out by impatient creditors and put up for sale the following spring. Undaunted, Mansfield arranged the sale of track and equipment to the new Sandy River Railroad, and the elfin 12-ton engines began hauling passenger and freight trains into Phillips during November 1879. "Light railways" had officially arrived in Maine.

Down at Bridgton, railroad talk became the principal topic. An intelligence unit was dispatched to ride and inspect the new Sandy River line. As a result of its excellent impression, Mansfield was approached to assume the role of developer and promoter. He accepted, and moved to Bridgton in February 1880.

Although Bridgton was by now thoroughly insistent on conceiving a railroad, the choice of route remained undecided. The gauge issue was pretty well cemented by success of the 2-foot Sandy River, but route was another matter. There were basically four possibilities: *1)* Bridgton via Naples and Raymond to Saccarappa (now Westbrook); *2)* Bridgton to Portland, using the convenient towpath of the abandoned Portland & Oxford Canal; *3)* Bridgton to the A&StL RR connection at South Paris via Harrison and Waterford; and *4)* Bridgton to the P&O RR at Hiram. Although plans for the Saccarappa route progressed as far as the chartering of the Bridgton & Presumpscot River Railroad in February 1880, the prospect of immense financial requirements

5

brought an early halt to that scheme. Faced with this barrier, the Bridgton delegation visited the managements of both the P&O and the A&StL in January 1881 with the hope of obtaining direct financial support. Spurned by both, the committee ordered its attorneys to draw up a revised charter, this time for a new railroad straight into Portland. Thus checkmated, the P&O offered to compromise by sharing freight and passenger rates on a fifty-fifty basis with the new company if it built to Hiram, located on the P&O line 36 miles northwest of Portland.

The Portland-direct advocates were led by A. G. Bradstreet, a prominent resident of Bridgton acclaimed locally as a "civil engineer of no mean repute." Claiming that the P&O-Hiram route was adverse to the best interests of the town, Bradstreet, along with F. H. Brown and G. S. Farnsworth, persuaded the February 28, 1881, Town Meeting to vote 365 to 53 in favor of a $40,000 grant to survey a route to Portland. This new charter eliminated Saccarappa and followed a slightly more northerly route via Windham, Gorham, and Deering, but the canny town fathers had also set a time limit, naming May 28, 1881, as the final date which Bradstreet was to have raised sufficient funds to build the railroad by his proposed route. This gave him just ninety days to rustle up an estimated $250,000.

Working quietly in the background, a rival committee pushed for the Hiram route. Join us, they said, and not only will the railroad cost less but a fifty-fifty revenue split with the P&O will bring early profits. The name they selected for this enterprise was Bridgton & Saco River Railroad.

On March 11, 1881, Bradstreet had published and distributed his *Proposition for a Railroad* in time for the third special Town Meeting concerned with what was rapidly becoming Bridgton's favorite wintertime topic of conversation. The P&O, perhaps hungrier for local revenue than before, rose to the occasion and invited the new company to lay a third rail if the Hiram route was approved. With the third rail, narrow-gauge trains could use P&O tracks clear into Portland. But despite frequent private gatherings and a big public mass meeting for a finale, the Bradstreet Committee was forced to admit defeat on the May 28th deadline. It was also Bradstreet's swan song among the pines and ponds of Bridgton. Within a month he packed off to Colorado Springs to sample the magic of 3-foot-gauge railways to the Pacific.

By 1881, ill effects of the post-Civil War boom and depression had worn away. Immigrants from Europe poured in by the hundreds of thousands, and the nation's population exceeded fifty million for the first time. American industry prospered temporarily under a protectionist tariff, and the stock market churned into new high ground. Among the limited fields for investment in those days, railroad stocks and bonds were quite popular, and small wonder when profitable railroads such as the New York Central & Hudson River RR were able to report 50 percent operating ratios. Even smaller companies, Maine Central for one, were doing well. Operating ratios of under 60 percent had been achieved there, and the stock sold at twenty times earnings. Railroads were the space and technology stocks of their day, and even narrow-gauge won enthusiastic backers as an interesting new scientific technique.

THE TRUE WAY

Broad is the gauge that leads to death
           and thousands ride together there;
But wisdom steers the "Narrow Gauge"
           The safer one for Travelers.

Then rouse thyself and take the prize!
           For 'tis just now at thy command,
And Nature's gifts to us are lost
           'Til we possess the Hiram land.

The wand'ring man will tire and faint
           Who waits for "Strait Route" any more;
And be esteemed—ALMOST—a saint
           If he rejects the open door.

Courage! Nor are our hopes in vain,
           Create this town almost anew,
By binding her with iron chains
           To masts through which our riches flow.

                           W.H.H.

1882

While history has not recorded how George Mansfield survived that first year in Bridgton, his estimate for building a 2-foot-gauge railroad, when finally requested, came through loud and clear. The price would be just under $9,000 per mile, and the operating cost was projected at two-thirds that of a standard-gauge railway. Transporting loads from one gauge to another, he argued, would cost less than the additional bond interest payments of the more expensive standard gauge. Broad backs were cheaper than greenbacks. Still another sales feature was that eventually the big railroad line would take over the small one at a fancy profit to investors and then widen the rails to standard gauge.

In those days innocent of telephones, radio, and automobiles, distributing printed handbills was a strenuous but often effective method of disseminating news and opinion. Pamphlet-printing must have been a most profitable sideline for the *Bridgton News* that year, judging from the volume of publications. The Hiram hustlers composed a document titled *An Appeal for the Bridgton & Saco River RR,* and the Bradstreet boys, not to be outdone, brought out *A-PEEL against the Bridgton and Saco River RR.* The *Bridgton News* carried frequent dispatches about the battle. Its editor, Major H. A. Shorey, chronicled each sortie in the florid style of the day, and for avid B&SR fans there was obvious delight in each editorial line when it was possible to announce on June 3, 1881, that the Bradstreet route was defeated and the way to Hiram was clear.

E VEN WITH BRADSTREET himself gone, the fight was far from finished. Still carrying on from North Bridgton was F. H. Brown and the stagecoach interests. On September 9, 1881, an injunction was delivered to the Bridgton town treasurer preventing the exchange of municipal bonds for any kind of securities issued by the Bridgton & Saco River RR. The charge was made that the Town Meeting had not legally authorized this exchange. In fact, by January 1882 the injunction was made permanent, pending more specific instructions from Town Meeting. Delay followed upon delay, and pamphlet tumbled after pamphlet. *Read This Without Fail Before Voting* was annexed by *Another Boomerang! The Last Desperate Struggle of a Desperate Cause!* Even the *News* got into the fray, with a Special Railroad Supplement vigorously supporting the earliest possible approval of the narrow-gauge railroad. It was a field day for pamphleteers. A large, articulate citizenry attended Town Meeting on March 6, 1882. Moderator J. T. Jenner proclaimed the tally. The vote was 553 to 175 in favor of advancing $36,000 toward purchase of 720 shares of railroad stock. It was a crowning victory for the Hiram Route supporters. The P&O RR bought 100 shares of stock and signed a 20-year rate agreement. Freight and passenger rates would be shared on an equal basis, but the smaller road would assume the cost of transferring freight at the Junction.

In retrospect, one could yearn for the projected Bradstreet route, utilizing the long straightaway of the canal towpath as a high-speed road to the Portland deep-water docks and connections with large railways. Even the route from Bridgton to South Paris on the Grand Trunk Railway should have succeeded, serving numerous towns along its projected 22-mile way. The road actually taken was the easy one, quickly financeable by lumbermen and supported by the P&O in its unceasing quest for new revenue sources. And no matter about that, for a most fascinating toy railway it surely became.

The first survey stakes were hammered in "as the snows lay in the hollows." Engineer Stephenson worked his party south from Bridgton until he came to an intersecting point on the P&O about a mile and a half below Hiram. Here beetle-browed Mount Cutler rises up above the dark pools of the Saco River, dammed by a jumbled outcrop of rocks several miles downstream. Exhausted from its steep climb along the Saco, the P&O track sought rest in wide, sweeping curves, and just south of Hiram it crossed the river on a long bridge. Near this bridge, an interchange yard was leveled and a small station labeled "Bridgton Junction" was erected.

The B&SR route managed to escape most signs of habitation or commerce, preferring communion with brooks, ponds, and pine trees. It even managed to avoid passing through the center of South Bridgton, a hamlet on a hill. This omission enraged the South Bridgtonians. In an effort to placate them, the railroad surveyed an alternate right-of-way through town. Its gradients were obviously too steep even for narrow gauge, though, and this "Soothing Syrup Route" was not built.

One of the most indignant potential customers bypassed was J. R. Foster, known as "Uncle Joe," who operated a sawmill, a gristmill and a shook shop, owned a store, and did a good deal of business with the outer world from a base called Foster Mills. According to Clara Berry, a lifelong resident of South Bridgton who was a little girl when the B&SR was being surveyed, "Uncle

9

Joe swore a mighty oath that never an ounce of freight would come over that despised road for him. 'I'll haul freight from Japan with a rooster, first,' he vowed. He was never driven to that ex-

Armed with a temporary spark-catcher, No. 2 pauses with its fresh-varnished train where the new roadbed had neatly parted a Cumberland County cornfield

pedient, but he never used the little road, either."

For many years the inconvenient South Bridgton station stop was little more than a lonely depot on a forgotten side road. Resi-

dents of the hamlet bitterly nicknamed the railroad the "Narrow Gouge," and their resentment lingered long.

Track was spiked in place throughout the fall and winter, and by January 12, 1883, the construction train chuffed into the little sawmill village of Sandy Creek. There was cheering in the streets and a volley of musketry by way of celebration: more rail and crossties—only a few more miles to go. The remaining gap was closed in little more than a week.

By the time the railroad reached Bridgton, its first two locomotives had already become familiar to local rail buffs, who had ventured down log paths and country roads to watch track construction. The twin engines came from the Hinkley Works in Boston, with tall, straight smokestacks, perhaps in honor of the stovepipe hats worn by President Lincoln. After a few months and several forest fires, small diamond stacks with screening were attached to chasten hot sparks. When better coal was available though, the diamond stacks vanished, and the little engines became more conventional again.

These 15-ton machines were 0-4-4 tank types, which meant that there were four drivewheels beneath the boiler and four wheels supporting the water and coal tank, all on one frame. It was an efficient design perfected by Mathias Forney, a mechanical genius with offices at 173 Broadway in New York City, a few doors north of Wall Street. The design was eagerly pounced on by locomotive builders seeking something suitable for narrow-gauge railroads, then springing up like daffodils after a spring rain. Among its distinctive features were a brass bell mounted above the sand dome and a graceful round cab roof with a raised center portion.

Rolling stock consisted of two wooden passenger coaches, a caboose, ten flatcars, and five boxcars. There was a "wedge" snowplow, assembled by the P&O shops as a welcoming gesture, and a "digger" car for plowing out snow between the rails. Turntables just long enough for the engines were installed at each end of the line. A two-stall engine house was built at Bridgton, and next to it a long two-track car shed, designed to shield coaches against sun, rain, and snow. At first there were separate passenger trains and freight trains, but after the initial thrill of train-riding and a fury of freight shipments, business died down, and each train ran with a mixed bag of freight and passenger cars. The extra engine had to perform ballasting chores until track was fully lined up and settled into place.

According to paeans of praise in the local papers, the 45-foot coaches were masterpieces of skillful construction. Their designer

*Forney Tank No. 3 tops off a head of steam preparatory
for another journey to the Junction*

at Laconia Car Company, in New Hampshire, was probably influenced by the Philadelphia Exposition of 1876, with its devotion to Gothic Revival and "stick" styling. Fittings were of polished and varnished brass, and included ornate oil lamps, coat hooks, match strikers, and door and window locks. Carved oak adorned the walls and window frames. Seats were of fancy cast iron and soft mohair, pleasing to the touch and yet durable. The coaches were named *Pondicherry* (Bridgton's earliest name) and *Mt. Pleasant,* in honor of the local high hill (now a popular ski resort). After the sand-and-gravel ballast had become firm and the wood trestles filled in, the little trains scooted along at 30 miles an hour, much to the delight of *Scientific American,* which sent a reporter to chronicle the innovating railway.

The Bridgton & Saco River Railroad's charter of July 1881 authorized the use of both debt and common stock to finance the fledgling project. Foreshadowing Artemus Ward, the Maine philosopher, the directors decided to "all be happy and live within our means, even if we have to borrow the money to do it with." Twenty-year 6% first mortgage bonds were issued in the amount of $80,000, and 1,800 shares of $50-par common stock were sold in the sum of $90,000—a total of $170,000. It was a new high in tycoonery for Bridgton; the borrowing even exceeded funds on deposit at the Bridgton Savings Bank, surely a commentary on the contemporary high regard for railroad securities as a vehicle for savings. The friendly P&O, as noted earlier, bought 100 shares of stock. In order to finance rolling stock and provide some working capital, $20,800 of 6% second mortgage bonds were offered. Precise final cost of the roadway was $166,035.74, in addition to $26,013.39 for rolling stock, totaling $192,049.13. For about $10,000 a mile, Bridgton owned its own railroad at far less cost than a standard-gauge line and for not much more than George Mansfield's estimate. Mansfield could return home to Boston with a feeling of rectitude, if with nothing more tangible.

The first board meeting was convened in June 1883. It harbored most of the town Establishment. The new president, William F. Perry, was manager of the Bridgton Machine Shop, makers of waterwheels and machinery, and of the Forest Mills Company, spinners of "cloakings and fancy cassimeres." Joseph A. Bennett, proprietor of Bennett's Hall and First Selectman, became secretary, assisted by C. H. Burnham, of a well-known local merchant family, as treasurer. As was typical of the day, prominent citizens hedged against fickle fortune by having more than just one occupation. Perley P. Burnham, one of the new directors, was chief engineer of the Town Corporation and also dealt in dry goods. W. A. Stevens manufactured wood staves and shook in his sawmill, and on Main Street he purveyed hardware and kitchen supplies. Owen V. Gibbs, an émigré to New York, was the only non-Bridgtonian on the railroad's board, but relatives of his ran the fine-woolen-making Pondicherry Company, not to mention the local savings bank and the Sebago Steamboat Company. Surveyor Stephenson was retained to supervise track maintenance, and Millard ("Uncle Mel") Caswell was master mechanic, assisted by John Marque, graduate of the Sandy River line.

Year-round rail transportation brought two important changes to Bridgton. One was that mill owners, backed by Massachusetts capital, could expand the woolen and shoe shops in Bridgton, and the other was that, with the broadening new concept of the summer holiday, Bridgton commenced to grow into a resort.

Inbound traffic was made up of soft coal for the mills and hard coal for house-heating, grain for horse and cattle feed, and virtually every article of merchandise and food not produced locally. Outbound traffic consisted of manufactured wool from the various mills, lumber products, apples, and other agricultural produce.

The price for goods and services had not increased as fast as population, and farmers and smaller manufacturers yowled lustily as freight rates were hiked upward. The rise in rates was brilliantly engineered by the powerful railroad trusts, and, in turn, Bridgton and Saco River revenues rose steadily. It meant that two or three new freight cars could be added every year; in fact, it was an opportune way for "Uncle Mel" to keep shopmen busy all winter long. The big Portland Company works supplied all necessary castings and forgings for hometown car manufacture in those days.

By 1892 there was sufficient cash surplus to purchase a third little steam locomotive. The new No. 3 came from the Portland Company and was similar to the first two successful engines, a similarity not surprising since Portland had acquired parts and patterns from the old Hinkley Works of Boston. Sister Forneys were ordered by the Sandy River, Kennebec Central, Monson and Wiscasset lines, and two of them, including this one, were going strong forty years later. The No. 3 wound up its career on the long, sinuous grapevine of the Wiscasset, Waterville & Farmington in an abrupt fashion. While piloting the down morning train one day in 1933, it broke a rail and plunged suicidally into the Sheepscot River, derailing part of its train and providing the *détente* for ceasing operations thenceforth.

During summer months, traffic conditions justified three round trips daily, inspiring for the railroad the local nickname of "Bustle and Scoot Round." When business receded in winter and the extra engine was needed for logging or for snow-bucking, two round trips sufficed. P&O's two daily round-trip trains made it possible for Bridgtonians to rise early in the morning, spend several hours on business or shopping in Portland, and still arrive home that very day for a late supper. In 1893, a total of sixteen thousand souls took passage over the Narrow Gauge, a thumping tribute to the travel habits of tourists, itinerants, and patent-medicine drummers of rural Maine.

Electric tramcars were then beginning to clang their way down city streets and into suburban communities. As a means of transport that was cosily warm in winter, airily cool in summer, and relatively unchallenged by mud, light snow and other climatic aberrations of the Maine climate, trolley networks successfully spoked out in all directions around the major and minor cities. In fact, the Westbrook, Windham & Naples Railway, a Portland Railroad affiliate, was issuing bonds and making noises about extending its Westbrook electric line all the way to Harrison, following the west shore of Sebago Lake and Long Pond. For persons with a high bile count—like Joe Bennett, who by this time was B&SR secretary-general manager-superintendent-freight agent-passenger agent—it brought pardonable anguish. (As Temple Critenden put it, Bennett collected jobs "as a magnet does tacks.") The railroad's board was called to meet the new challenge.

On Bennett's insistent urging, surveys were made, land was purchased, and permission was obtained during the winter of 1897 to build a 5½-mile branch from Bridgton to Harrison. The new line "Y"-ed east from the mainline a half-mile south of Bridgton Depot; passed the Pondicherry Mill with its new sidetrack for coal unloading; and curved north past the Farmer's Exchange, crossing Stevens Brook on a long steel-girder bridge. The 35-pound rails dropped downgrade as they pushed northward toward the western shore of Long Pond. Curving north and east around the lake, long wooden trestles and earth fills led the Narrow Gauge past rural North Bridgton to the sunny shores of Harrison. A turntable, a two-stall engine house, and a comfortable mother hen of a station were constructed. Barely months after the initial spadefuls of dirt, the first little train squeaked and smoked its way into the new terminus on August 3, 1898. The trolley bluff had been called, and copper wires were never strung north of Westbrook.

To obtain the $35,000 needed for expansion, the Lilliputian company sold $10,000 in stock and raised the rest through a refinancing operation. To extinguish $106,000 of 6% first- and second-mortgage notes still outstanding, a new 4% consolidated issue of $125,000 due in 1928 was authorized. A few years later, when further funds were needed for new cars, locomotives, and rail, a second consolidated mortgage of $17,000 was vended. Masterfully, the company had built a new branch, refinanced its debt to a far-off maturity date, and emerged with lower interest costs than before. Was the new branch a financial success? By the addition of only 25 percent more track, profits were enhanced by nearly a third.

Meanwhile, down at the Junction, new track was being laid to keep up with the solid volume of lumber, coal, and heavy articles of freight that kept a full-time interchange crew of three or four men working steadily. For its part, Maine Central, scion of the old Portland & Ogdensburg, countered with another track and a

B&SR No. 2 scampers across the long trestle into Harrison yard

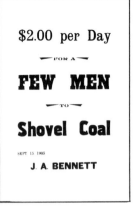

turntable. Thanks to the spurt in profits, the Toy Railway embarked on an equipment spree, adding locomotives, baggage and passenger cars, a second snowplow, and several larger-capacity freight cars. A tiny tank car to haul kerosene was put together from an iron tank and an old flatcar and later on, when motor cars were all the rage, a second and larger tanker was put on to satisfy the growing thirst for "gasolene," as it was then spelled. The tank cars were actively used until the early Thirties, when the Portland distribution terminal quit the rails in favor of more flexible highway trucks.

The "middle period" of motive power ushered in three new teakettles, urgently needed to assume the heavier burdens of passenger and freight traffic. The first of this series was the No. 4, another 0-4-4 tank engine, built in 1901 by the H. K. Porter Company of Pittsburgh. It was similar to, but slightly larger than, the first three. Perhaps its best claim to fame was a dome, or steam fountain, located inside the cab. This furnished an unintentionally excellent cab-heating system, so that the No. 4 was preferred for logging and snow-bucking duties in winter. A less pleasant memory is of No. 4 waddling down the track during a summer rainstorm, water pouring down the gap between dome and cab roof, creating an unwanted and unloved sauna bath for the engine crew.

No. 5, which arrived in 1906, achieved a sort of fame during its busy and adventurous years on the B&SR. The engine was obtained from the Portland Company, a diversified "conglomerate" of the day, which made boilers, machinery, and elevators, as well as railroad equipment. Possibly the fact that Master Mechanic Caswell's son was a designer at the works helped clinch the order; more likely, the nearness and the consequent saving in shipping costs assisted in the decision. The No. 5 was the first of the Toy

Nearly-new No. 5 pauses for a pose at Harrison

Railway's motive power to have a swiveling set of front wheels. This pony truck greatly aided the "tracking" qualities of the engine, as well as spreading the increased weight over a longer wheelbase—No. 5 was five tons heavier than its predecessor. The No. 5 was unquestionably "good-looking," as engines go, and it became the regular passenger locomotive. Speeds on the Narrow Gauge were usually 20 mph or less, but on one particular trip the boys apparently decided to try for a record, and fleet-footed No. 5 came close to hitting an unbelievable 50 mph.

No. 5 was also caught in the B&SR's most serious accident on record. On bright spring days, shimmering track can become hot as a rash, so that rail expands, and only needs vibration to throw itself loose from the crossties. Between Ingalls Road and Perley's Mill, where the track clung to a high roadbed over rugged, swampy terrain, No. 5 came humming and drumming up the hill with the morning "mixed" from the Junction. As it drew near, the rail kinked and twisted, and No. 5 and its first two cars turned turtle. The fireman leaped for his life, but engineer Roland Woodbury clung to the brake ejector valve, hoping to slow the derailed train. The derailment had thrown the engine too much to one side for this action to be effective, however, and it toppled down the steep bank. Although badly scalded, Woodbury was able to crawl to safety. Two days of jacking and timber-blocking righted No. 5, and in due course of time it received new jacketing and a replacement wooden cab.

No. 5 was the very last steam engine built by the Portland Company, which evidently found paper-mill machinery more profitable, so next year the Narrow Gauge turned to Baldwin in Philadelphia for No. 6. It was similar to No. 5 in general appearance and was ordered jointly with No. 16 of the Sandy River, which may have accounted for its bargain price of $5,600, only a few dollars more than Portland's price for the smaller No. 5.

No. 6 was a valiant component of the "Boston Excursions," which had begun in 1898 with completion of the Harrison Branch. Trainloads of genteel Bay Staters would buy combination tickets between Boston and Harrison, arising at dawn to entrain for Sebago, where steamboats would require most of the day to churn their way up Sebago, through the Songo River, and north through Long Pond to the landing at Harrison. Here No. 6 or No. 5 would lie in wait with every available piece of passenger equipment, including an open-air excursion car. Men, women, and children, picnic baskets and all, would then make a headlong rush for the narrow-gauge train, which, as soon as loaded, would make a mad dash for the Junction and the long, dark train ride home.

Bowlered and bearded Joe Bennett, iron man of the strait gauge, now presided over a highly successful enterprise. By 1907, thirty

In happy days early in the century, Baldwin No. 6 preens
before the Bridgton engine house

Songo River steamers "Goodridge," "Bay of Naples," "Songo," and "Worrambus," the mail boat, frequently met the Narrow Gauge

thousand passengers produced $17,000 of annual revenue, and $7,500 more came from mail, express, and baggage. Freight accounted for 47 percent of total revenues. The Toy Railway's operating ratio was 72 percent that year, only slightly inferior to the Maine Central's, although somewhat superior to that of the less efficient Boston & Maine. An important factor was that the Narrow Gauge charged higher rates than the big roads: for example, it cost 3.4 cents a mile to ride on the Narrow Gauge, against 1.8 cents on conventional lines. Another factor was wages, which were about 20 percent less than those paid on the "Broad Gauge."

Compared with the rather uncomplicated company organized in 1881, the 20th-century B&SR by now had become a busy, complex enterprise. Train movements, passengers, articles of freight, locomotives, and even problems proliferated with the passage of time. Two regular crews were kept busy attending to four round-trip passenger and mixed trains during the summer months. There were forty-four employees on the payroll. Most of the live-wire founders, such as Bennett, Hall, Burnham, Walker, Fuller, and Young, were still officers and directors, but old age was advancing upon them.

Meanwhile as tourism and the lumber industry grew, so did the ambitions of neighboring Maine Central. It looked around to diversify. Hotels, steamboats, and branch-line railroads offered excellent promise, particularly if joint freight and passenger rates could be achieved and if accounting and mechanical supervision could be centralized.

Ever since opening day of the B&SR, Portland & Ogdensburg and its successor, Maine Central, had owned 100 shares of B&SR

Powerful No. 7 pops off in the Junction yards

stock. By June of 1912 the Maine Central's treasurer's office had been able to round up a total of 2,045 B&SR shares at a cost of just over $100,000, and took over control of the Narrow Gauge. The then-outstanding $170,000 of 4% bonds remained in private hands around Harrison and Bridgton.

Maine Central's first steps to modernize the line were capable and professional. For example, the chief engineer's office found a discrepancy of several hundred yards in the road's alleged length, so that the former 21.09 miles became 21.25 miles. Mileposts were installed, replacing country-road crossings, bridges, and even large rocks as reference points. Maintenance was stepped up, so that the whole line was resleepered. Rails of 48 pounds in weight, said to have come from Maine Central's Rockland Branch, supplanted all remaining 35-pound mainline rail below Bridgton. Stations were repainted in Maine Central pond-bottom brindle. Enamel station signs appeared.

Most important of the outward signs of progress was the arrival of engine No. 7, a handsome 2-4-4 tank architected in 1913 by Philip Hammett of the Maine Central, the Baldwin Locomotive Company, and "Uncle Mel" Caswell, the short, sharp-eyed doyen of the B&SR mechanical force. To accommodate No. 7, another stall was built at Bridgton and a machine shop was constructed, using lumber from the vacant Perley's Mill station and the old car shed. Joining well-proportioned No. 7 was a new passenger-smoking-mail car and three 34-foot boxcars, veritable piano crates compared with the snuffbox cars previously available. Now passengers in Portland could purchase one Maine Central ticket all the way to Bridgton or Harrison, and it was as though the Narrow Gauge

21

Giant Maine Central No. 510 dwarfs the ageing No. 5 in the Junction interchange yards

Train and transfer crews line up for photography with reliable No. 6

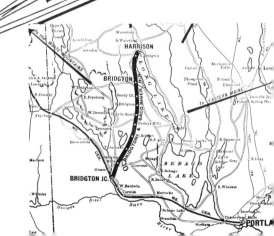

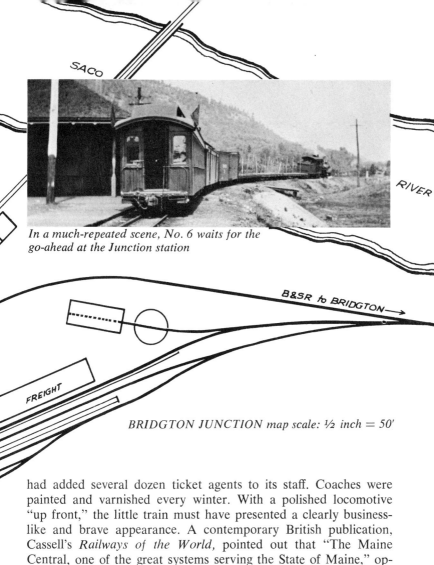

SACO

RIVER

In a much-repeated scene, No. 6 waits for the go-ahead at the Junction station

B&SR to BRIDGTON →

FREIGHT

BRIDGTON JUNCTION map scale: ½ inch = 50'

had added several dozen ticket agents to its staff. Coaches were painted and varnished every winter. With a polished locomotive "up front," the little train must have presented a clearly business-like and brave appearance. A contemporary British publication, Cassell's *Railways of the World,* pointed out that "The Maine Central, one of the great systems serving the State of Maine," operated the B&SR and Sandy River as "lines of high class construction and equipment—miniature reproductions in every respect of the parent." Cassell's editors had studied narrow-gauge railroading in India, Africa, and South America, and it was indeed difficult to ignore praise so broadly knowledgeable. When No. 7 and its rake of deluxe coaches eased out of the Junction yard beside the sparkling waters of Saco River, it must have registered as an unforgettable memory in a traveler's railroad experience.

The Great War brought a surge of prosperity to the B&SR, a situation that lasted, however, only long enough for postwar labor

The Saco River sometimes made a pond of the busy Junction yard

and competitive problems to develop. In 1921, high-water mark of the Toy Railway, revenues were inflated to $112,000, of which $80,000, or 70 percent, was from freight. Net income was $23,000, indicating a profit margin of 20 percent. Equally impressive was the balance sheet, suggesting a prosperous small investment trust rather than a bucolic branch line up in Cumberland County, Maine. Government bonds were listed in the amount of $50,000, in addition to cash of $11,000. Total assets of the 21-mile company were $378,000, a rather encouraging bookkeeping achievement, equal to about $18,000 per mile. A year later, some of the Treasuries had been redeemed and replaced by $10,000 of 5% Boston & Maine bonds. The mortgage lien of $170,000 still remained, and in view of the low interest coupon, it is probably not surprising that the Maine Central treasurer saw no reason to retire them.

Thus armed with cash, the company ordered another new locomotive from Baldwin, similar to No. 7. It was delivered in 1924. In addition to being the line's largest engine (38 tons compared with 15 tons for the original machines), it was also the last 2-foot-gauge engine built for stateside common-carrier service. A rounded steel cab lent No. 8 a rather modern, muscular appearance. According to Ernest Ward, former employee and author of *My First Sixty Years,* No. 8 was the Narrow Gauge's most powerful engine, having once lugged nine loaded freight cars and six passenger cars from the Junction, Everett Brown driving. Roland Woodbury, another regular engineer, coaxed a record 14 cars of coal with No. 7. Assuming a maximum of 12 tons per car, however, the entire

24

*No. 6 and No. 4 nudge the old wedge plow for yet
another mile of heavy snow*

train was equal to no more than three standard-gauge 55-ton hopper cars. Perhaps more cars could have been towed uphill if two engines had been used, but no doubt the strain would have been too much for the aged wooden car frames.

In a region where four or five months of snowfall are not uncommon, the new, larger engines were a blessing when it came to snow removal. The traditional system had been to hitch two or three small engines behind a wooden wedge plow and buck out the drifts. It was often a race against time when snow was wet and the thermometer played leapfrog with freezing. Crossings and switches had to be picked and shoveled by hand, since the smaller engines could not crush their way through the accumulated ice. The bigger engines with their higher drivers, greater steam pressure, and heavier weights could urge a steel nose plow down the line even after a heavy fall. The morning plow train would often leave with either No. 7 or No. 8, together with caboose No. 101 and flanger No. 40. The flanger performed two duties, one of which was to plow out between the rails, the other to push aside waist-high snow with a wing plow. As Linwood Moody, laureate of the Narrow Gauge, put it, old snow was shoved aside to be ready for the next fresh fall of snow. Sometimes the wedge plow was towed along to help widen the pathway through the drifts, since pushing the plow often resulted in derailments—not the most desirable form of excitement at below-zero temperatures.

Snow was only one of the major harassments.

By 1925, economic and technological conditions brought about a total reversal of fortunes for the miniature railway. Improved

25

highways and the lack of general improvement in railway facilities accompanied a refocus of travel habits. Utilizing the charter of Sam-O-Set Hotel Corporation, Maine Central sent deep-cushioned twenty-nine passenger Fageol buses thundering up U.S. 302 to serve Bridgton and Harrison. Simultaneously, B&SR train service was cut back to one steam train per day. That train left at a discouragingly early hour of the morning, and usually chuffed back to Bridgton with two or three loads of freight and a car of express and second-class mail. Engines No. 7 and No. 8 formed the backbone for regular service, with No. 6 as the spare; No. 4 and No. 5, unable to pass inspection without repair, were quietly retired.

From a fat balance sheet and robust profits five years before, B&SR results ebbed to a deficit of $6,000 in 1925. It was a humiliating departure from the happy days of 1912, when Maine Central could boast that "the property is entirely self-supporting, has paid regular dividends for a number of years, and furnishes us with traffic of considerable value." In 1926, the B&SR suffered the first financial embarrassment in its history: its bond interest fell into default. Worse, someone coined the nickname "Busted and Still Running" for the little road that had once borne the admiring label "Bustle and Scoot Round."

There was no longer a Joe Bennett to raise a clamor or to press charges, and his successor, Everett Crosby, was not inclined to play the statesman. In July 1926 a mass meeting was held in Bridgton—recalling the stormy days of the railroad's birth—and practically every person in the Maine Central, from President Morris McDonald down, was taken to task. Claiming deliberate sabotage, the citizens sought counsel and decided to retake their railroad. By this time, the Maine Central was in no financial condition to fight back.

Perhaps if the entire bond issue had been purchased and then extinguished by the larger company, a speedy end of operations

No. 5 and No. 6 break through the drift after a particularly grueling blizzard of the Twenties

The first day of Bridgton & Harrison Railway operation was hexed by this bizarre derailment near North Bridgton

could have been predicted. However, Bridgton bondholders came to the rescue. They formed a new corporation, called the Bridgton and Harrison Railway, and in March 1927 the group was granted its charter to take over "Busted and Still Running." Receivers were appointed, and within three months funds were pledged by the town government and by prominent citizens to purchase a required amount of common stock in the new corporation. In effect, ownership returned to Bridgton for a mere $27,000. The package included 21 miles of track, three good locomotives, and 60 cars. The Maine Central, meanwhile, wrote off its $100,000-plus common stock investment as a dead loss.

On June 12, 1930, the Bridgton & Harrison Railway Company officially assumed jurisdiction over the 21-mile railroad, and that very evening No. 8 and a two-car train jumped the rails and capsized between Harrison and North Bridgton. Unhappily, Maine Central had never upgraded the 35-pound rails on the branch, and 38-ton No. 8 fell victim to a rain-softened sag in the roadbed. The locomotives and cars were easily rerailed, but the mishap forced a hard decision on the fledgling management. Because lumber and canned-food traffic from Harrison had declined drastically, and since people were traveling by motor car if they traveled at all, the branch was stealthily abandoned later that year. No longer did the Bridgton & Harrison Railway run to Harrison. The limb that might have become an interesting Maine scenic attraction years later was cut off in the interest of bodily survival.

A second step in home-rule retrenchment was construction of a homemade gasoline railcar for passenger, mail, and express

27

*Innocent of paint or polish, the diminutive Baldwin No. 6
vacuum-brakes its mixed train to a halt at the
Harrison terminus during latter Maine Central days*

← TO BRIDGTON

LONG LAKE

*An unhurried scene at the Harrison station finds
the morning train amid a small welter of chicken crates,
mail wagons and weedy sidetracks*

service. Gasoline section cars had been chattering up and down the Narrow Gauge for over twenty-five years. The first car was designed by Section Foreman Hibbard; another one used a Palmer

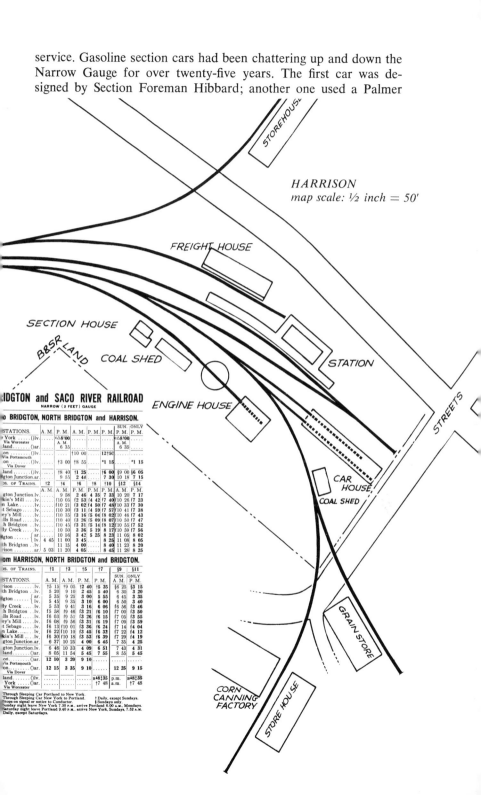

engine intended for boat propulsion. For his own sport and conveyance, General Manager Bennett captained a peppy 2-cylinder, direct-connected Fairbanks Morse inspection car. In summer he commuted to Bridgton from Hancock Pond; his attractive cottage was located brief yards from the water tank. These light track cars were prone to derailment and consequently sallied forth with spikes, angle bars, and track tools more useful as ballast than as implements. There was a Model "T" track auto that was officially No. 1. It carried the mails in times of emergency.

Drawing upon this fecund background, the B&H created in 1930 a mechanical monster, the like of which has never been seen before or since. The most recognizable component of the new No. 2 was a 1927 Chevrolet sedan, but from there on, the viewer was on his own. The tonneau was suspended over three axles, and a single axle box trailer clung on behind, craftily supported by the third axle that was in effect the power drivewheel. The heavier the load in the boxcar, the better the traction. For many, this Chevrolet "bus" was a first introduction to the grassgrown ways of the Narrow Gauge. And it was usually an unforgettable introduction. The cadence of the four closely spaced sets of wheels over the rail joints set a vigorous tempo for the trip, accompanied by the kettledrum beat of the roaring motor as the "bus" chased up and down the many hills en route. It possessed a fire siren borrowed from the Bridgton Fire Department; at each road crossing the piercing wail was sufficient to set woodchucks scurrying long before the thrashing machinery clattered into sight.

The tatterdemalion "bus" seemed to symbolize the plight of the Narrow Gauge during those belt-tightening days of the Depression. It was a period when small railroads and trolley lines were failing at a fearsome rate. Except for the Monson Railroad, which survived as a service outlet for a famous Maine slate quarry, all other narrow gauge in New England had vanished. Even Maine Central's morning train from Bartlett to Portland disappeared, and the agreeable option of making a day-long business or shopping trip by train was perfidiously taken away. By all rights, the B&H should have closed, but dogged determination kept it going and insured that mail, express, freight, and even passengers could arrive by train if desired.

Except during the summer-camp rush, seven men were the staff. Maurice Heath, who had grown up in the office under Joe Bennett and Everett Crosby, was general manager, devoting his day to writing express company invoices and igniting a stubborn pipe. Everett Brown, master mechanic, tinkered in the small shop, taking outside machine work from time to time to provide extra

30

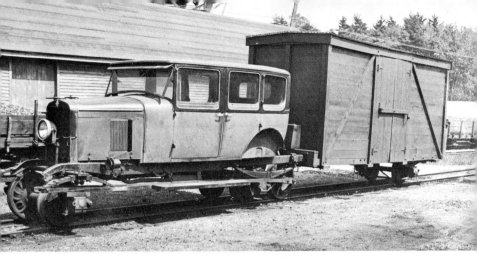

*Bridgton & Harrison's answer to depression conditions was
a self-propelled bus shown here at Bridgton between runs*

income. Walt Mackey presided capably over the Junction yard,
and Roy Staley, George Sargent, and Leon Trumbull alternated
between track chores and assisting with the freight train. There
was also the railbus job, and a more punishing assignment was
never thought of. Walter Brown, Jr., Kip Gammon, Leon Trumbull, and at least a half-dozen others alternated over the years at
driving the "bus." At stake was a vigor-sapping twelve-hour day,
starting when Train No. 1 departed close to 7 A.M., and ending
when Train No. 4 limped home at 7:12 P.M. On occasions the
steam train sauntered forth with the morning run and the "bus"
handled the afternoon trip. More often it was just the gasoline
unit, piled head to toe with express packages, mail sacks, and as-
sorted freight. From 10 A.M. to 4 P.M. the bus driver loaded a

*Under declining Maine Central fortunes, B&SR No. 7 coasts
into Harrison with a near-empty train*

light Ford rack truck and raced with parcels all over town. On the seventh day, a rest cure was advisable.

During 1936 the wonderful Sandy River & Rangeley Lakes Railroad was rent asunder. A casualty of the age, its main line and branches were torn up, excellent freight cars burned for salvage, and stylish narrow-gauge engines junked for lack of another user. Everett Brown made a trip to Phillips, Maine, and looked longingly at the narrow-gauge toy store being dismantled.

There were engines No. 9 and No. 10, similar to his own No. 7 and No. 8, which would have fitted into the numerical structure of the B&H, and also have offered several years of repair-free operation. At $250 each, they would actually have been cheaper than a new set of tubes. But B&H was short of cash, with wage payments often in arrears until the welcome mail or express check arrived at month's end. Given a paltry $1,000 and travel money, B&H could have re-equipped itself with new engines, new coaches, and new freight cars, all in sound condition and, better still, provided with efficient air brakes.

There was one piece of equipment the B&H really wanted. It was a high-wheel, modern-looking gasoline railbus built by the Sandy River shops under Master Mechanic Stinchfield. And on November 13, 1936, H. E. Salzberg Co., scrappers of the SR&RL sold railbus No. 4 to a schoolboy of fifteen who offered it to keep the Narrow Gauge operating. Although the bigger railbus, No. 5, was first choice, it had already been sold, lamented Superintendent O. M. Vose. This left the smaller, three-axle machine, which was used almost to the end of operations, hauling flatcars of loaded scrap rail to the broad-gauge connection at Farmington.

The new railbus, thereafter loaned to the B&H for $1 a year,

Railbus No. 3 with its pick-a-back trailer waits for the afternoon mail delivery and a downhill glide to the Junction

was hastily trucked to Bridgton, given a new coat of brown paint, and provided with a four-wheel boxcar trailer. To conform with the local numbering system, it became No. 3. The metal cowcatcher was removed until summer, and a pair of small snowplows were attached to the front end. Built originally as a four-wheel Reo railbus, it was later given a four-wheel front truck, and the single drivewheel was powered by a throaty Chevrolet truck engine with four-speed drive. A single-tone trumpet truck horn was installed, and without any prior intention in the matter, it evoked the image of a midwestern interurban electric car. The new "bus" had the advantages of speed and power; life was made simpler for its hapless driver.

The car was economical to operate, as periodic reports from the delighted general manager, Maurice Heath, bore out. His venerable Underwood, chattering like a man with loose storebought dentures, chronicled every perfection of the new railbus. Once in a while, however, someone would forget to fill the tank, and the "bus" would trickle to a halt, inevitably a mile or more from the nearest telephone. Then the Ford truck armed with a five-gallon can would come dusting down the corduroy back roads, ever mindful of a furious postmaster in Bridgton who grew progressively less sympathetic to delays of this nature. Barring minor encumbrances of snow, rain, and occasional motor spasms, the new "bus" proved itself a vital acquisition, and was in fact formally praised by the Board of Directors as the savior of the railroad in its most difficult period. On occasion it was the "official car," as when the public-utility inspector came to visit, and one time, at least, it teamed up with the old Chevrolet "bus" to tow a carload of freight when both steamers were laid up with leaky flues.

BRIDGTON YARD became a minor beehive each June when the boys' and girls' camps came alive. Some of the camps—Accomac, Winona, Wabunaki, Wigwam—had been in business for many years, and they remained steadfast customers of the railroad. Campers called it "The Dinky," and regarded each travel experience with well-behaved glee. When the big Maine Central train clanked into the close quarters of the Junction station, a tide of faces, with a rush and a roar, engulfed the four narrowgauge coaches. At least a few railroaders wondered whether it wasn't as much business savvy as loyalty on the part of the camp directors to patronize the railroad, since baggage was checked free with the passenger ticket. The baggage often arrived on an express car a few days later. It took a special steaming of the engine and a back-creaking day transferring heavy trunks from one car to the other.

Beginning with a small stream of rail buffs in the middle Thirties, a torrent of fans eventually flowed into Bridgton to view the "famous and unique two-foot-gauge railroad." Amateur press agents popped up from Maine to California. Bridgton became a regular venue for aficionados from every corner of North America. Large and small groups chartered the train. Local inns frequently organized jolly charter outings of one sort or another. By far the outstanding achievement of public-relations gimcrackery occurred when six rail fans from Worcester hired B&H for $60 a day. The story, picked up by an observant news syndicate, appeared in more than three hundred newspapers, thrusting Bridgton and its offbeat narrow gauge upon the national scene.

Typical of more ambitious trips was the annual Boston Railroad Enthusiasts Excursion, which gained enough popularity by the close of the Thirties to justify its own locomotive and coaches clear through from Boston. In 1940 the Boston tour leaders apparently failed to inform Bridgton of the strength of the crowd. As it was, all coaches and two "observation" gondola cars had been aired and swept for the occasion. When the broad-gauge train arrived at the Junction, however, a panic of people besieged the narrow-gauge train. Every seat was occupied, and after two

Fan trips and camp specials echoed the halcyon days when No. 7 tugged six coaches over the narrow gauge

*Excursion days brought camera-laden railbuffs
and double header trains*

empty coal cars had been commandeered, several score of fans
rode the car tops, an alternative that, despite soot and sparks, was
undoubtedly the preferred seat assignment on a sparkling, sun-
drenched July day.

If the Narrow Gauge was an unusual type of operation, it was
also a safe one. Accidents were minor rather than major. The
normal mishap was a derailment due to spreading rails. On one
occasion, when No. 8 was returning home after depositing two
hundred giggling girls at the Junction, four coaches fell between
the fence-wire rails on a long curve, miles from the nearest road
crossing. It was a damp area where, as Rogers Whitaker might
put it, spikes were pressed resolutely into the woody moss of the
crossties. It took a full day of ticklish maneuvering of 10-ton car
bodies, jacking and replacing the crossties under them in a kind

TO HARRISON →

35

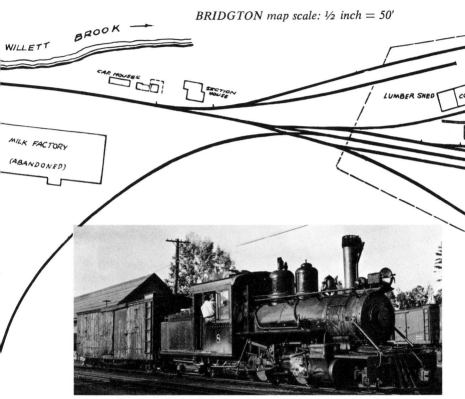

WILLETT BROOK →

CAR HOUSES

SECTION HOUSE

LUMBER SHED | COAL

MILK FACTORY

(ABANDONED)

*Everett Brown and No. 8 shunt a loaded boxcar
in the freight house sidetrack at Bridgton*

No. 7 was a suitable ornament for the ancient Bridgton engine terminal

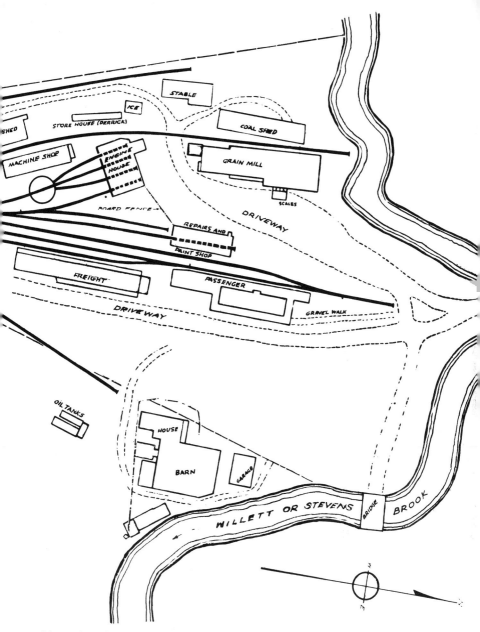

of herculean balance act, to set the Narrow Gauge on its feet again.

With the exception of No. 5's famous dive in 1911, few wrecks of the road made newspaper headlines. A common disablement was that of snowplow trains heading into the pine stubble after glancing off a packed drift, or derailing at a road crossing choked with ice or mud. A costly wreck of the 1920's occurred when No.

Frost heaves play hob with No. 7 near Rankin's Mill one fine spring day

7 swung around the curve from Harrison and slam-banged into combination car No. 25. No. 7's front end had to be rebuilt, and the new number plate and cut-down handrail totally changed the engine's facial expression. The splintered end of the faithful combine was rebuilt, but with a cargo door on one side only, a feat of legerdemain rendered possible by the particular location of station platforms relative to No. 25's usual position in the train. No. 25,

Rerailings took time, muscles and lots of wood blocking

baggage car No. 30, and car No. 101, nicknamed "The Buggy," were unsung heroes of the line and undoubtedly earned more profits than any other three cars of the Maine narrow-gauge network. Near-accidents numbered in the dozens, to judge from the last decade of operations. Baggage car No. 30, with a low coupler on one end, was prone to disconnections, and the vacuum-brake system was so delicate that the engine's reverse lever was with great dependability used as a braking tool down hills and in switching operations. On one excursion, a parting of the coupling resulted in a coach's drifting backward from Deep Cut for perhaps a mile before it was retrieved. (A playfully tipsy passenger was suspected.) Low speeds and care on the part of employees doubtless prevented many a disaster. With pure hearts, each had the strength of ten.

During the summer of 1940, No. 7 was retubed, and its drivewheels were machined to a track-worthy contour. Old tubes were cut with an acetylene torch, and new ones were sized, fitted, and rolled tight by hand. There were 125 fire tubes, each accorded care and precision. After the reworked drivewheels had returned from the big machine shop of the Portland Company, they were unloaded and rolled to a vacant engine stall. Here was a drop pit, as dark and gloomy as a medieval torture den. A grimy electric bulb hung from the rafters like a lonely vigil light. Around the soot-spangled walls were hooks, barbs, and iron instruments used in extracting truth from narrow-gauge men and equipment. Like ungainly dragons, looking enormous in their cavernous lodging, the two engines lurked. The only sounds came from drips of water, and, for all one knew, Abbé Faria and young Edmond Dantès lay gasping in a corner, plotting escape. Everett Brown, as head armorer, had prepared the setting better than he knew.

The great iron wheel was coaxed onto a heavy screw jack, which was supported on an ingenious four-wheel cart, mounted on its own set of rails down in the torture pit. The man selected to be wheel-broken submitted to crawling down into the Stygian blackness, where decorations were the rotting small bolts and nuts of old machinery. When the screw jack was depressed, and the big wheel had dropped by several feet, the small tram made its half-rod pilgrimage to a position immediately beneath the 35-ton monster for which the wheel was destined. As though a crude necromancer had been at work, a large portion of the lower anatomy of the engine had been dissected, leaving an opening for this visceral wheel.

39

To the exhortations of the chief armorer, the apprentice murmured a silent prayer of appeasement to the iron dragon above and commenced ritual elevation of the massive wheel. Quarter by quarter the big screw jack was turned, and the wheel obediently rose to its union with the great body above. The apprentice, crammed into a cul-de-sac in the masonry abyss, turned the screw cautiously. The higher the 5-ton wheel moved into its crenelations above, the more the chance of its wobbling and making a total sacrifice of the new apprentice.

New apprentices usually survived, but the engine house was the scene of many tourneys and joustings. The battle of the hydro test pump was a favorite contest. Here, the apprentice was placed in a pit of gloom and given a small force pump. When the handle was pumped smartly, pressure built up in the water-filled boiler to test against leaks and cracks. At the other end of the field of honor was a perpetually leaking set of fittings. The object of the tourney was to pump fast enough to create more pressure than the leaky fittings released.

When No. 7 was back in service, and after a sampling of cars had been painted by vacationing admirers, busy days of 1913 were recreated, when there were new engines and cars and, better still, heavy loads to handle.

On one particular late-summer day, the camps were moving out, and the heating coal was beginning to move in. It was the perfect stage for a tonnage demonstration. As the scene opened around 6:15 P.M., No. 7 had just discharged a suntanned cargo of young ladies at the Junction and the mothering Maine Central had clasped them to her bosom, anxious to speed them to their pallid big-city haunts. Passengers for Bridgton were a dozen uniformed counselors, a handful of rail buffs, and a crew of regular employees and summer helpers.

To point the train in the opposite direction to return to Bridgton required intricate maneuvering. Step One was to back the entire train from the Junction station for several hundred yards to a slope. Step Two was to set hand brakes on the train, those on the first two cars usually being sufficient. Step Three was to coast the locomotive downgrade and into the freight yard. Step Four was to turn the switch, release brakes on the train, and let it coast down the main line past the freight-yard lead switch. Here the train would be parked until the engine was serviced.

Down in the yard, the engine drifted to a turntable, almost hidden by the tall field grass. It was a small steel turntable, shrouded in wood, and came from Harrison when that branch was

Heavy repairs and modernization were carried out at the Waterville Shops under Maine Central tutelage. This visit of the early Twenties yielded an electric headlight system

abandoned. Two men could turn the engine, placing their backs against the coal-tender end and walking backward, digging their heels into the yielding sand. On a short stub track was a barnlike one-place engine stall with a ventilator on top and a water tank inside. Here, if the old one-cylinder gasoline motor was in good humor, a tender full of cool water would be taken on. The Junction water supply had always been subject to various inventive approaches, and at one stage a steam ejector was provided for lifting water directly from a well sump. Later a second-hand Chevrolet motor was brought in when the one-lunger gave up forever.

Easing carefully over the turntable track, where gaps between rails could be measured in inches, the engine would steam back to a coal-loading shed. Covered against Maine winter snows, as everything had to be, the shed could contain a broad-gauge car of coal unloaded from a short section of double-gauge track. The coal thus unloaded would be spooned into wooden tubs of 500-pound capacity, which were moved up and down the shed by a tiny 2-foot-gauge tramroad. A hand-operated windlass, creaking piteously when in use, would lift loaded coal tubs from the tramway to the locomotive tender. It was a simple matter to up-end the great wooden pail in a cascade of coal dust and shiny ebony chunks. The same coal was used by the Maine Central, and until B&H was forced to buy piecemeal truckloads of slack, wonders in steam could be performed.

The ritual of coal-loading was accompanied by a mysterious process known as soot-blowing, or cleaning the front end. The fireman, who knew this part of the liturgy well, would first open two orifices in the smokebox, a round chamber beneath the smoke-

41

stack. He would then twist open a small valve, which sent clouds of steam from the opposite side of the engine. With a long iron wand, hidden until this occasion, the fireman would next poke around in the smoke chamber, like a dentist probing a swollen gum, until an accumulation of cinders was sucked out by the steam jet. The steam made a noise like a subway train, and the effect was equally terrifying. A third part of the boiler ritual was blowing down the boiler, which involved tweaking another concealed fitting so that dirt and scrofulous corruption were purged from the steel monster's insides in a torrent of roaring steam.

The yard itself consisted of four narrow-gauge tracks, which permitted a cat's cradle of car movements. At the lowest elevation of the yard was a transfer facility for gasoline. In another area where the standard-gauge track was high, grain could be chuted down into narrow-gauge boxcars. On level stretches, coal could be shoveled from one car to another adjoining. One dismal track at the side, a victim of scrapping, retained only rusty fittings and charred remnants.

The little engines were capable of impressively fast acceleration, and the vacuum-brake-cum-reverse-lever provided acceptably fast stops. Switching routines were uniformly brisk. The vacuum ejector, with a distinctive muffler mounted on the cab roof, would shoot columns of steam upward when the brake was applied. It sounded like the gasping of a cleaning-and-pressing establishment. A system of hand signals, peculiar to the Narrow Gauge and innovated before contemporary memory can recall, was used to indicate which track would be attacked next in sequence. The rapid routine doubtless had its start when four or five trains a day cluttered the Junction yards.

When the train was made up, it would back up to the station so that a baggage car or boxcar could be loaded with less-than-carload freight, which typically arrived in scandalously bad condition from the big road's way-freight car and sometimes sat for days until the steam train made its run. The engineer would use this loading period to polish and oil around, a relatively simple task at a most convenient height, even for a short gentleman. It was like capturing for a brief moment the glory of 1913 when No. 7 was ready for its triumphal homeward march, accompanied by many followers and much baggage.

The "highball," or go-ahead signal, was normally the dirty-gloved wave of George Sargent. Two peremptory toots of the steam whistle were followed by the sucking, oozing, hissing sounds of steam applied to mechanical motion. Slack in the nine-car train ran out with a series of uneven bumpings and clunkings, soon supplanted by the keening sound of the wheels gaining their way on the gently rusting rails. The deep, hollow chuff-CHUFF-chuff-chuff of the exhaust gained in tempo as the engineer took advantage of a slight sag. As the train clattered over the freight-yard switch, the exhaust shouted faster and louder. Two miles of 2.5 per cent grade were immediately ahead. At the East Hiram crossing, still within sight of the Junction yard, the engineer sounded an urgent whoo-WHOO-whoo-whoo. Motor cars, happily, were scarce on these back roads.

Up through the cut around the base of Small's Mountain the little engine pounded, its clanking and quick-paced chuffing echoing off the sidewalls. Pine-tree branches that had dared to grow too close to the roadbed were tossed skyward by the miniature volcano heaving its protesting load uphill. Passing by Kennett's Siding, in East Hiram, the engine pulsed more confidently, and the engineer eased off his reverse lever. Exhaust beats became more distinct. The sun had been spreading an agreeable warmth among the fields, and the scent of pine boards drying in a lumber-mill yard blended with the distinctive hot-oil smells of the laboring locomotive.

Now the railroad picked up Hancock Brook, which it was to follow for several sylvan miles. As the train crossed the Hancock Brook stonemasonry arch, heavy cinders rained down on the mill-pond like a sudden mountain storm: the fireman was feeding the monster's appetite. On it labored, past Buttermilk Falls and two crossings at Rankin's Mill, which were saluted by the full orchestra of whistling. Rankin's Mill, long bereft of its watermill, had shrunk to a tiny hamlet on a lonely country road. The road crossing was a difficult one, subject to wash-ins after thunderstorms, and the cause of more than one derailment. A mile of following the twisting trout brook brought the narrow-gauge train to "The Summit," about 500 feet above sea level and nearly 150 feet above the Junction, 2.5 miles south. Here was Mullen Siding, where northbound and southbound trains passed each other in busier days.

As the engine reached this summit and achieved more level terrain, the safety valves let go with a shuddering volley. Using this valuable reservoir of steam, the engineer opened a steam valve and pulled back on an injector lever, forcing fresh water into the steam boiler. Within a minute, the steam-driven injector had consumed the extra pressure, and the safety valves subsided without dissent. The tenor of No. 7's injectors faintly resembled a gathering of Scottish pipes playing a repetitive dirge. The injector had other noises too, such as a drumming protest when

Squealing around "The Notch" with Everett Brown, engineer, and George Sargent, fireman, during the minor revival of the Forties

the cold-water supply was dwindling, or internal rumblings when steam pressure was too low.

For what always seemed an interminable stretch, the train rambled its way through a lonely area of second growth. Here and there were relics of a forest fire several years before, and visible through the rotting stumps and underbrush was Barker Pond. Beside a mossy trail was a tiny station shelter with one of Maine Central's big enamel signs proclaiming "Twin Lake." Occasionally a nearby camper would flag the train there to post a letter, but like much of the narrow-gauge line, Twin Lake station mainly served the convenience of small animals and birds which nested in its rafters.

Crossing over a woodland stream, the track began to climb again. On the right-hand side at milepost 5 was a gravel pit, used once in a while by track crews to provide ballast after washouts. During the colder months, the fireman, when he rested after stoking the fire during this upward climb could make out the ice-covered surface of Hancock Pond. The engine's exhaust grew firmer as the grade steepened and the train slowed. Many short sections of rail with deep drivewheel burn marks testified to the steepness of this section. Moments later the pounding machinery's echoing off rock walls proclaimed "The Notch," nearly six hundred feet above sea level. It was often dusk when the evening train reached this point, just as

> The lonely sunsets flame and die;
> The giant valleys gulp the night.
> The monster mountains scrape the sky,
> Where eager stars are diamond bright.

One evening when the headlight system unaccountably failed, a young engineer, weary after many hours of work, mistook "The Notch" for another hill, forgetting the sharp slope on the north that whipped the tracks down to water level at Hancock Pond. Only the engine had its vacuum brakes attached that night, and as the heavy coal train weighed down on the small locomotive, the engineer blew for brakes, but the men in the "buggy" thought it was the usual toot for a deer or a raccoon. The wheels locked, and sparks like Roman candles erupted from the sanded rail. Opening the cylinder relief cocks, and cautiously bringing the reverse lever into rearward position, the young engineer abandoned the vacuum brake and left the cylinders to act as a brake. The throttle valve leaked enough steam to provide further braking effect.

Cy Warman must have experienced moments like this:

> Oft when I feel my engine swerve
> As o'er strange rails we fare,
> I strain my eyes around the curve
> For what awaits us there. . . .

The flickering, faltering glow of the ashpan gleamed on unfamiliar ferns and young hemlocks as No. 7 sped down the track, with the long curve below. Who had any right to expect that this old bag of bolts would successfully round the turn? Still, by a hair's breadth, it did.

The route lay along the verdant east bank of Hancock Pond for nearly a mile. In Narrow Gauge days, summer camps and a scant dozen cottages ringed the beautiful lake, with its view of Allen Mountain to the west. During the heyday of operations, tiny steam trains passed each other on a long sidetrack, and there was a spring-fed water tank at which Bridgton-bound trains habitually stopped. New tenants of Joe Bennett's Hillside cottage shared the spring, and during August droughts heated words were

45

known to be exchanged between cottagers and train crew, understandably concerned when only a foot of water filled the cavernous wood tank.

West Sebago, 7.2 miles from the Junction, consisted of a dusty road crossing and a passenger shelter. Inside was a magneto-operated telephone, permitting conversation with the terminus. It was the usual instrument for reporting derailments, tieups, and other disasters. Out of consideration for the local postmaster, who met all trains at West Sebago, engineers and bus drivers tried to be as punctual as possible. Without fail, the postmaster would be seated at traintime in his aged Model "A," baking in the sun or chattering in the cold. When the train approached, his spare old frame would emerge with a thin, worn mailbag, West Sebago's contribution to the literature of the outside world.

Two miles beyond was Perley's Mill, now nothing more than a grass-covered sidetrack. The section crew used it as a port of refuge to escape the mainline train. Also, when the track gang was nursing the aftereffects of an especially impious evening, Perley's Mill sidetrack was therapeutically invaluable.

Between Fessenden Hill and Fitch Hill, the Narrow Gauge ascended another hump. Swamps, streams, and small ponds dotted this enduringly rugged countryside, and deer, foxes, woodchucks, and partridge were often encountered as the train nosed around sharp curves. Ten miles from the Junction, the little train ground over the Ingall's Road dirt crossing, whistling compulsively and bell-ringing to greet a lone motorcar, which by a precise coincidence in eternity had chanced to pass this way. The old, weather-beaten "T"-shaped RAILROAD CROSSING sign leaned at a perilous angle.

Near by was The Deep Cut, another of the hilltops, a long cutting through a ledge, now lined with rows of small hemlocks.

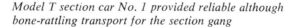
*Model T section car No. 1 provided reliable although
bone-rattling transport for the section gang*

At Hancock Pond tank, No. 8 takes on water, with a trio of coal-filled boxcars in tow, during a cold February day of 1941

Along this bucolic stretch of track, with rails and telegraph line the only reminders of civilization, there was a cold spring right beside the roadbed. The spring had bubbled in the middle of the survey line, so construction crews piped its ice-cold water to a mossy enclosure of stones. Although not on the timetable, Cold Spring was a regular stop for nearly every summertime train with a moment to spare.

The engine now drifted downgrade, its huffing accelerated as the tracks followed Willett Brook, which eddied and flowed northward to join Stevens Brook and Long Lake. Sandy Creek, 13.6 miles from Bridgton, no longer harbored a sawmill, and the grassy side-track was no longer guarded by a station house. Farmer boys, fishing for pickerel in the millpond, waved eagerly as the engine whistled and smoked its way through the miniature community.

Three sturdy sectionmen—Brown, Staley and Hibbard—pose by the section house at Hancock Pond tank

With his charge's siderods flailing and valve gear urging a faster beat, the engineer took advantage of the descending grade. The track was straight and true, and where it followed U.S. Highway 302, the Narrow Gauge accepted its one supreme challenge to show off speed and style. Looking back over his train like a sergeant dressing off his troops, and being assured that all cars were present and accounted for, the engineer brought the reverse lever up to its highest gear, pulled the throttle another notch, and whistled long, loud, and commandingly for the Willett Road crossing. The obedient click-click, click-click over the loose rail joints was most audible as the train rolled forward toward the last mile of line. Road signs, filling stations, and houses on small plots of land here betokened the outskirts of Bridgton-on-the-Lakes. As No. 7 passed the former switch for the Harrison Branch, with its once-lucrative traffic sources, a long whistle blast was set off to declare the train's arrival. Safety valves were popping, and the vacuum-brake pipe became alive with steam, recalling tens of thousands of similar entries and arrivals since days of 1883, nearly sixty years before.

No. 7 vacuum-braked its train to an easy, soundless stop, and then, with energy born of experience, the train crew crowded into action, manning couplers and switches in precise order so that the engine could cut off, run forward, stop, and then back down past its train to the tune of its quick-step, hollow-voiced, distinctive narrow-gauge exhaust beat. At Bridgton, the engine was always immediately turned, so that it could switch out its train using the tender coupler, which was a safer arrangement for the switchman. Coal cars were shunted down a long, curving supply track, usually after ten or twelve protesting empties had been coaxed out of the rusty spur. Drivewheels would spin until a switchman could find the inevitable car with its hand brakes tightly clamped shut. Coaches would be returned to their dormitory track, and other loads would be bullied, shoved, and thumped into appropriate niches of the yard.

After losing its hotbed of coals to the ashpile, the locomotive would crawl contentedly into its engine-house compartment, to simmer and gurgle in sleep until stars were brightest in the cool Maine night.

For the young apprentices who spent their college vacations helping the Narrow Gauge, the work was a vigorous stewardship of antique equipment and declining business. As a service concept, the Narrow Gauge was no better than its connecting links, and when main line service became progressively less flexible, it was love of the rails as much as rates and service that kept volume as high as it was until 1940. On their annual visits, mail and express officials miraculously confirmed their contracts, and Harold Morrison, a director and prominent coal-and-grain dealer, regularly vowed his intention to support the Narrow Gauge.

THERE IS A CHAPTER in most railroad history books dealing with the shabby wind-up of operations. Usually the scrapman gets the track, the truckman takes the traffic, and the town residents keep the memories—and little else. The Toy Railway's final chapter was similar—but with a completely unusual twist.

Bridgton, as it struggled out of the Great Depression, grumbling at the Roosevelt administration every inch of the way, was, for all its quaintness and Maine-ness, tremendously affirmative about the future. The tatty old mills were being reopened. Paint and publicity were being applied to attract bigger tourist crowds. Mount Pleasant, supplied with reliable snow, gave promise of becoming a great ski resort. City folk were beginning to invest in lakeside property. It wasn't quite a boom situation, but Bridgton was eager to move ahead.

It was apparently Bertram D. Scott, a Democrat and chairman of the Selectmen, who led the first campaign for abandonment. On October 25, 1939, at a sparsely attended town meeting, it was decided by 60 to 53 to instruct Judge Pike, town clerk, to vote the town's railroad 10-year-old stock interest in favor of abandonment at the December railroad meeting. Further, the town meeting decided to accept a price "in excess of $20,000" for the railroad. Leading the pro-railroad forces was Selectman C. Lester Ames, also a prominent local Democrat, president of the railroad. In a spirited series of letters and speeches, Ames defended the railroad, predicting that it could become a tremendous tourist asset to Bridgton in the years to come. Moreover, with some 20% of the town budget allocated to welfare, closing the railroad would escalate the burden. Ames wisely pointed out that the cash proceeds of the abandonment would have to be applied to reduction of town debt rather than directly toward a new school or a ski resort, as some naively believed. Robert C. Braun, a receiver of the railroad during the year after its bond default, countered that the railroad was of "no economic value whatever" to the town, and that without heavy expenditure, serious wrecks could occur.

At a director's meeting soon afterward, the town action was repudiated, but at a special town meeting on December 7, a vote of 149 to 103 upheld the previous vote to sell. Two weeks later at a stormy railroad stockholder meeting, this action was confirmed, and a Portland agent by the name of James V. McNutt was appointed to carry out the sale. Apparently McNutt made no effort to reach or develop possible operating groups, and with a swiftness almost too rapid to be coincidental, he revealed that a Newburyport junkman, Benjamin O. Checkoway, had deposited cash toward a selling price of $20,001, just one dollar over the asking price.

The railroad directors, however, unanimously refused to sanction abandonment, which Checkoway required to tear up the rails. Instead, they issued a proclamation that business was improving and that continuation would serve the public interest. The "destruction crew," not to be outdone, called another special town meeting on May 6, 1940, and instructed Edgar F. Corliss, secretary of the railroad, to apply for abandonment with the Interstate Commerce Commission. Under Docket No. 12878 hearings were scheduled for 10 A.M. on October 10, 1940, at the Federal Court Building in Portland. Meanwhile, Checkoway, through his attorney, Raymond N. Evans, threatened a lawsuit against the town unless the road were abandoned forthwith. Over forty persons attended the hearing, requiring the use of a larger room than originally called for. Lester Ames, the president, hotel owner James C. Chute, former General Manager Charles R. Dodge, Dr. Asaph Walker, a director and vice-president of the road, and numerous shippers and passengers testified in favor of the line. Scott of North Bridgton, traditional home of opponents to the road, and Claude P. Meserve testified to the run-down condition of the road, brazenly taking issue with the Maine Public Utility Commission which had rendered a favorable physical report after its most recent inspection. Doughty Judge Pike, town clerk, was by this time counsel for the "destruction crew;" William B. Nulty of Portland represented the "opposition."

In December, 1940, I.C.C. Examiner Thomas F. Sullivan proclaimed in favor of abandonment, and, as of January 17, 1941, the formal certificate was granted. The gist of the decision was that the railroad had served the purpose for which it had been built and that it could not compete with modern highway transportation. Thus washing its hands of local controversy, and ignoring possibilities of continued operation under new sponsorship, the matter was closed as far as Washington was concerned. Weeks later the Maine Commission meekly rubberstamped the Federal action.

At the last sad railroad meeting on a sunny day in February, 1941, Dr. Walker, Harold E. Morrison, Maurice W. Hamblen, Sam Gallinari, Harold G. Braithwaite, Lester Ames, and Bert

Scott were elected directors, with Lester Ames as president and Ed Corliss as clerk and secretary. Maurice E. Heath was reappointed general manager.

By this time, the news shock of abandonment claimed wide attention. Even the town residents began to have second thoughts about closing down forever. The problem was, money was scarce and those who possessed it acted tongue-tied when approached about purchasing and rebuilding the line as a tourist proposition. The single bona fide group interested in purchasing the line, headed by Cornelius Schaible, a New York advertising executive, was thwarted by Checkoway. He refused to sell his option, back out, or make any kind of concession. He even paid up the entire price by July 1 when threatened by the directors. Not ready to quit, the Ames armor went into action again and called another special Town Meeting on July 18, 1941, to see if the Town would be willing to sell its five-sevenths interest for $12,500 instead of $15,000. By a 37 to 5 vote, it was decided to sell to an operating group on the basis that the group would have to settle with Checkoway. Individual stockholders would retain their interest. Every possible effort was bent toward locating a prospect. If a visitor arrived in a clean shirt, a necktie and a motor car of recent vintage, the railroaders would philosophize about gleaming prospects and golden possibilities for future operations.

A tall, quiet gentleman with a penchant for cigars came on more than one occasion to watch the steam train switching around the yard, and he would be observed waiting for it at key road crossings as it coasted through in a momentary swirl of dust and coal smoke. He had the biggest and newest car anyone had seen, and at length, inevitably, one of the railroaders asked him if he were at all interested in narrow-gauge trains.

At first he shyly said that he enjoyed visiting Bridgton because it gave him a certain sense of freedom and relaxation. He didn't mind driving two hundred miles from his home near Cape Cod to stand around the small town and watch the people.

The apprentice railroaders heartily agreed in this estimate of the situation. They too came from distant points, and enjoyed the anonymity of working as trainmen and mechanics after a winter of advanced physics, economics, or political science. It was indeed a halcyon period for these young men, who would live in converted boxcars at night, be awakened by firecrackers lighted by their friendly adversary, Erlon Brown, Everett Brown's prankish younger brother, and eat breakfast at 6:30 A.M. in a converted railroad-car diner managed by "Ma" Billedeau.

John Holt, one of the young railroaders, and the diplomat of the crowd, was assigned to escort the quiet gentleman on a special railbus tour of the line on a particular Sunday morning. The train could stop at various scenic places, and the splendid features of the Toy Railway could be explained at leisure. The object was to sell the railway lock, stock, and barrel for future operation.

The quiet gentleman puffed his cigar over the invitation and drew intriguing sketches on the backs of manila pads. But it was August, 1941, and the new friend returned to Massachusetts without further conversation. The tourists ran like lemmings back to their cities. The apprentices drifted away to their studies, and subsequently to the Army draft call that whispered just around the corner.

The last train ran almost without ceremony, old No. 7 puffing back into Bridgton for the last time on September 7, 1941. Then was the Narrow Gauge "all done."

Within weeks after the formal closing, however, it developed that the quiet gentleman had purchased virtually all of the rolling stock and equipment, except what the apprentice group had bought with their savings and borrowings. Ben Checkoway, the metal merchant, had scrapped virtually nothing. The rail went to the U.S. Navy, and presumably lent its weight toward defeating the enemy. The engines and cars sold for preservation were set aside in storage until the war ended in 1945, despite requests to use them on military railroads overseas.

The quiet gentleman, who turned out to be Ellis D. Atwood, of South Carver, Massachusetts, trucked locomotives, coaches, freight cars, tank cars, snowplows, flangers, shop equipment, and all manner of Bridgton railroadiana to his new Edaville Railroad, which had its roots in an extensive 2-foot-gauge tramway serving his vast cranberry plantation. Within a few years he had added equipment from the derelict Sandy River and Monson roads, and his shops became capable of building new cars from the ground up. Subsequently, under F. Nelson Blount, Fred Richardson, and David Eldredge, the Edaville became a full-fledged railroad, operating in summer and the Christmas season to the delight of hundreds of thousands of visitors every year. Edaville today has a world-famous narrow-gauge railroad museum, and its several other historical collections add to the culturally invigorating atmosphere there. The place is laid out as a park around a reservoir, which the railroad encircles. There are shady pine groves and picnic grounds, where people of every rank and station pay homage to Bridgton's Toy Railway. It has entered a new life, totally beyond the dreams of its founders and far above the fervent hopes of its Bridgton supporters.

The last slow train of October, 1941,
recedes rail by rail to the Junction, and little
remains to mark the course of 60 years

No. 7 and No. 8 on a postman's pension wheel hordes of tourists
on the famous Edaville line near Cape Cod. New or rebuilt coaches
match air brakes and brand new boilers for the engines

DATA and DRAWINGS

BRIDGTON AND SACO RIVER RAILROAD (Locomotives)

Number	Builder	Date	Builder's Number	Wheel Diameter	Cylinders
#1, 0-4-4T	Hinkley	1882	1563	30″	9x12
#2, 0-4-4T	Hinkley	1882	1564	30″	9x12
#3, 0-4-4T	Portland	1892	624	30″	10.5x14
#4, 0-4-4T	H. K. Porter	1901	2360	30″	11x16
#5, 2-4-4T	Portland	1906	628	33″	11x14
#6, 2-4-4T	Baldwin	1907	31827	35″	11.5x14
#7, 2-4-4T	Baldwin	1913	40864	35″	12x16
#8, 2-4-4T	Baldwin	1924	57659	35″	12x16

Notes: Automatic couplers and Eames vacuum power brakes standard equipment by 1900. Electric headlights fitted by 1920. Engines #7 and #8 equipped with outside mainframes, balanced slide valves and Walschaerts valve gear; others inside frames and Stephenson valve gear. All B&SR engines were "tank" engines with coal, water and boiler on same frame.

RAILCARS

#1	Ford "T" 0-2-2-0	Built by B&SR for inspections and roadway maintenance. Retired by 1940.
#2	Chevrolet "Six" 2-2-2+2	Built by B&SR after 1933 to replace steam train, later used for maintenance.
#3	Reo 4-2-0+4	Built by SR&RL for Strong-Kingfield service, purchased for B&H in 1936 by Supt. Mead, to Edaville 1941.

BRIDGTON AND SACO RIVER RAILROAD (Equipment)

Coaches:
#15—"Pondicherry" and #16 "Mount Pleasant"—built 1882 by Laconia Car Co., Laconia, N. H., 41 feet long, 28 passengers.
#17—Laconia, 1904, 42 feet 6 inches long, 29 passengers. Distinctive feature was double-paired windows surmounted by cathedral glass.

Versatility and utility were demonstrated when No. 6 towed oversize loads for a growing Bridgton

Boiler Pressure	Light Weight	Original Cost	Final Disposition
140#	15 tons	$3,000	Scrapped 1910
140#	15 tons	$3,000	Sold as WW&F #5 1912
140#	19 tons	$4,200	Sold as Kennebec Central #3 1920, later WW&F #8
140#	23.5 tons	$4,830	Retired 1927
180#	25 tons	$5,500	Retired 1927
180#	27.6 tons	$5,570	Retired 1935
180#	33.3 tons	$8,500	To Edaville 1941
180#	37.5 tons	$13,610	To Edaville 1941

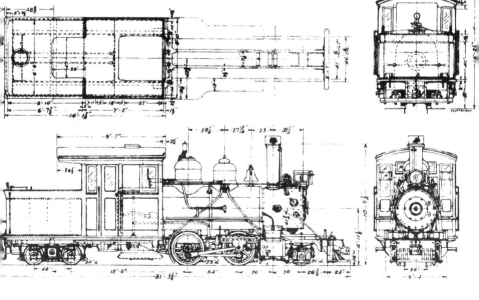

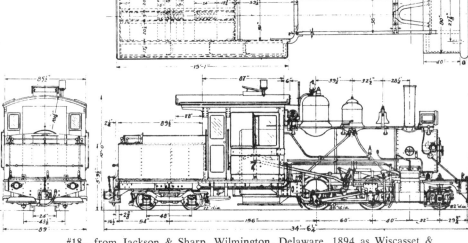

#18—from Jackson & Sharp, Wilmington, Delaware, 1894 as Wiscasset & Quebec #3, 39 feet 9 inches long, 29 passengers. Car purchased for $1,500 during one of the Wiscasset line's sinking spells in 1911.

#25—supplied by Maine Central RR 1913, possibly complete rebuild of earlier car from Sandy River system. Combination mail-baggage-smoking car. Seating capacity 30 persons. After numerous rebuilds, "The Smoker" sold as restaurant in Bridgton, c.1936.

#30—three-door baggage-mail-express car by Jackson & Sharp 1900 for B&SR as #11, 41 feet long.

#31—two-door baggage car by Laconia 1882 as #10, 41 feet 6 inches long.

Notes: Cars 15, 16, 17, 18 and 30 sold to Edaville. Car 30 dismantled, wheels and hardware reused by Edaville for SR&RL coach.

BRIDGTON AND SACO RIVER RAILROAD (Freight Equipment)

Flatcars: At one time as many as 40 cars numbered under 1913 MeC scheme from 44, the oldest, down to 2, the newest. Older cars 10 ton capacity (Laconia) and newer ones, built by B&SR, Portland Company, and Portland Terminal carried 15 tons. Width 6 feet 6 inches, lengths ranged from 26 to 34 feet. Cars weighed 5 tons.

Boxcars: As many as 30 were operated at one time, numbered from 45, an original 1882 car, up to 73, newest and largest car. Boxcars varied in length from 26 feet to 34 feet, heights from 8 feet 11 inches to 9 feet 5 inches overall. Cars averaged 7 tons in weight, capacities 10 tons for smaller and 15 tons for larger cars. Two 1882 cars in regular service as recently as 1941. Three largest cars constructed 1913 by Portland Terminal carshops.

No. 8 with the "Buggy" No. 101 await completion of repairs on baggage car No. 30 at Bridgton's small but effective "Paint Shop"

Until 1918 when the contract was lost, Smoker No. 25 housed a tiny railway post office where letters were sorted en route. Hugh Boutell, an early admirer of the Toy Railway, poses meditatively

Coach No. 15, epic of the carbuilding art, awaits the duty call

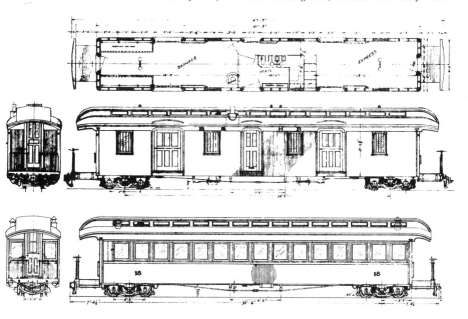

Tiny narrow gauge tankcars shuttled fuel to Bridgton's growing army of flivvers

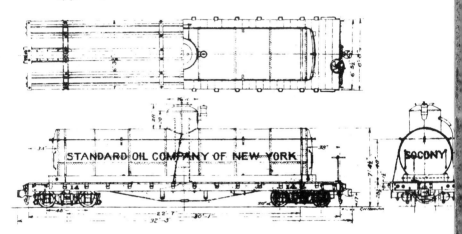

Company Equipment: No records describe flanger car (digger) built to order by Portland and Ogdensburg RR 1882; however, 17 foot plow #1 built 1882 lasted until Harrison Branch closure. Plow #2, 24 feet long, arrived 1898. Flanger #40 constructed on Laconia flatcar #40, extensively renewed about 1934. Caboose #101 built 1882 by Laconia, 31 feet 8 inches long, large sidedoor and two windows on one end. Caboose cupalo damaged by low guy wire and subsequently removed. Nicknamed "The Buggy", #101 served as combination mail-passenger car for many years. The B&SR operated for several years during the early 1900's, a center-bench open observation car built on a flatcar.

Tank Cars: Flatcar #21 built by B&SR 1903 provided with a tank for gasoline and range oil. A few years later flatcar #22 built by Portland Company 1899 fitted with a slightly larger tank. Both cars held as much as a small standard gauge tankcar.

Other Special Equipment: Certain boxcars with wooden shutters for ventilation were set aside for carrying grain. Most boxcars used for lumber, wool products and general freight, others for carrying coal in wintertime. Two small boxcars and four-wheel flatcar used with gasoline railcars. B&SR had usual complement of gasoline and hand-propelled section cars. Ford highway stake trucks used to make express deliveries in Bridgton area. B&SR boxcars, flatcars, tankcars, and special purpose cars sold to Edaville and in use as of 1968.